MINING Y♥UR SELF W♥RTH

CELESTE CRUZ

Dedication

This book is dedicated to my Grandmother Shirley,
to my younger self, and most of all to you reading this right now.

First Edition 2024

A LUBE FOR SELF-DISCOVERY

MINING Y♥UR SELF W♥RTH

CELESTE CRUZ

*"The deeper that sorrow carves into your being,
the more joy you can contain."*

The Prophet by: Kahlil Gibran

How do you know
if this book is for you?

Have you ever wondered why you end up in relationships that never seem to deepen or improve and have the same basic "challenges"? Have you ever suspected or been directly told that you don't hold the same beliefs about yourself that your family holds about you and did that produce a sense of shame or guilt? Maybe you just love reading self-development books. Maybe you are inquiring for a friend or you're curious about the concept of self-worth and how to relate to it. Or maybe you know without a shadow of a doubt that you really need work in this department and this book seemed like the low-risk option you could feel safe to start with.

All of those reasons are totally relatable and reasonable! Read on.

Contents

Contents

A Note From The Author

My Belief

I believe that we're all different versions of the omniscient, omni-present, omni-loving energy of life and creation. I refer to this source as God. You may have your name for what this represents for you. It's my belief that at our core, we are all illuminated by this source and that how we appear in our three-dimensional reality is the manifestation of creation in countless varieties with the agreement and purpose of life simply feeling itself, mostly this agreement is on a subconscious level. My views may be considered heady and psychedelic for sure.

We, humans, live in a complex web of communication that extends to and interconnects all of our generations and the rest of humanity. How all of this got started or where it's leading, I can't quite say. (Perhaps I can try exploring that in another book...) You need not believe as I do in general, nor do you need to share my beliefs to benefit from this book. I just think it's important for you to know my core beliefs and how they root my words here. Although I didn't write this book through a spiritual lens it is without a doubt spirit that led me to create it for you.

I wrote this book from a therapeutic lens of navigating codependency, parts work, somatic practices, positive regard, and a culmination of all of my work as a therapist as well as my work as a recipient of therapy. I have benefited from everything I will share with you. In short, I'm going to give you multidisciplinary and multi-sensory tools for your self-exploration, think of it like some lube for you to glide into your journey of self-discovery. You're welcome.

Nugget

To get the most out of this book, read it all the way through, then come back and read it for a second time with a journal and pen close by. Revitalize yourself through this process by means of taking a pause to put the book down if you need to then return with gentle courage.

You'll notice Nuggets sprinkled throughout the book. These are golden moments for you to deepen your process.

CHAPTER 1

How We Learn About Our Self-Worth

Learning about our self-worth is foundational. If you were a structure—let's say a home—everything about your structure would rely on the foundation for support. Self-worth is the very support that determines how (or if) the rest of your structure is maintained.

Self-worth focuses on the core of who you are within and has intrinsic value, while self-esteem primarily focuses on external factors like what you have or do in relation to what others have or do. Although these two concepts are different, they're interwoven into the fabric of how we internalize ourselves and move through the world around us.

Our Family Of Origin (or FOO) is where we receive our first messages on how to relate to ourselves and the world around us. This education comes in both explicit and implicit forms from the time we were babies, we began to absorb and apply what we needed to learn in order to survive in our environment. ("Environment" here being the people, places, energies, and things we're born into more so than our ecological or geographical climate.) The messages we received in the first few years of life helped inform us and helped us establish our self-worth and self-value within the world around us.

What we learned from our FOO may very well not be true, but we tend to believe it because we have no reason not to. Our FOO is our first and most impactful teacher and too often, an incorrect and very flawed one when it comes to learning about and understanding our value. This is why we can most often identify with some sort of generational trauma and/or codependency.

A note on codependency, at least from my perspective: we are all co-dependent to some degree. Humans need one another to survive, after all. However, when that need for connection thwarts the sovereignty of another, whether it's causing anything from mild discomfort to straight-up abuse, then the need for each other has become a tool of dis-ease rather than connection. Not being treated with the acknowledgment that you have inherent value and are deserving of love and respect can be traumatic in and of itself. For example, a lack of respect from someone who was supposed to be providing emotional labor for someone else—especially when that someone is a caretaker/parent may very well result in the disrespected person leaning to people-please as a form of connection.

Beyond our FOO, the secondary strengthener for how we relate to ourselves and the world around us is the dominant cultural beliefs and how they impact or strengthen the beliefs we already hold about ourselves.

With all of that in mind, let's look at some ways your FOO and society could have determined your worth for you:

Family of Origin

- Birthing order (this extends to you as well as to your parents'status in the family when they were children)
- Beauty/body type and physical abilities
- Cognitive abilities
- Emotional labor
- Gender
- Sexuality
- The ability to be shaped by and accept they family narrative

Society

- Social status
- Financial status
- Educational status
- Career
- Beauty standards
- Race, ethnicity, nationality
- Gender, sexual preference
- Cognitive abilities
- Political affiliation
- Religious affiliation

Sequentially speaking, once we determine/accept our worth—which is determined for us through our FOO story—then begin the journey of uncovering where and how we fit into the rest of the world around us. Where there's an overlap between our FOO-imposed beliefs and what society has told us, the interconnected stories of who we are and what our self-worth is strengthened and we believe those stories to be our Truth (with a capital T).

You may have noticed that some of the things listed above are mutable while others are not. For instance, a person can objectively change their job or even their appearance, thus gaining a higher worth status by society's standards, yet in their FOO they remain the middle child who frequently acted out and was subjectively considered to be unreasonable and not particularly attractive. This can create a sort of splitting in their identity, prompting them to show one face to the world and compartmentalize the "less worthy" (this is where shame shows up) parts of themselves in the shadows of their mind. (If they're held in too tight these parts can become neurosis but, that's for another book.)

The beliefs that a person can hold about themselves as a result of their familial input make it harder (this is where guilt shows up) to see themselves as being anything beyond the ingrained story. What's more, is that some people never look behind the labels they were given in childhood (because of guilt, shame, or fear or because they don't know how) unless the labels and beliefs attached to them begin to no longer feel like they resonate. For some this burgeoning awareness can feel like a curiosity meeting with discomfort; for others, it feels like being suffocated by the flames of a burning bush.

This discomfort usually propels people to go into over- or under-activated states and behaviors that lead to an unbalanced way of relating to themselves, people, places, and things. For instance, they may want to hide away from the world because they're sure they're going to be hurt, or they'll be tempted to drink or shop their feelings away. Or maybe they'll hone in on someone else, thinking, "This person will become my new best friend/lover and I'll focus on what's happening in their life so that I don't have to look at my own." Usually, these coping behaviors are not obvious to the person but sometimes they are. Can you relate?

On their own, taking time to yourself, shopping, having a (m)cocktail, and making connections with new people, on their own are not "bad." It's when these things are sought after from a place of fear, a lack of self-worth, denial, or self-abandonment that they extend past their balanced and even necessary purpose at times and extend into becoming personal red-flags. I want to validate that wherever you are on this behavioral spectrum, you're likely uncomfortable, and from my perspective, all self-awareness is good.

Why? Because awareness precedes change and you have the power to change. If you can self-identify with splitting, it is survival, it is not bad, it's your intelligence working for you. At one point, your brain determined that in order to maintain safety, and oftentimes that meant "fit in" to the family system, certain parts of yourself had to be hidden away or cut off. The more you can see this as a coping skill, the more compassion you can cultivate for yourself and for the choices that you've made to get you to this point in life. That's not to say a great deal of grief and anger are not also present. Feel those emotions too. But as soon as you can, lean into your compassion.

Safety is important to recognize because safety can mean sovereignty, which is the ability to be yourself at any given moment in your childhood. You may relate to the word "safety" immediately because your household was indeed a scary place with blatant physical or emotional harm. Imagine if you had always felt unsure about what would happen next or if you had felt a sense of needing to be on alert. Or if you had felt pressure to be/act in certain ways so as to avoid being criticized by a parent or sibling.

Self Inquiry

Your FOO (and let's face it– society, too) have so many stories about you, the family system, and how it should run. These stories are well established and some have been cultivated for generations. Allow these questions to prompt you to dig deeper and think about where these stories might have originated.

- What brought you to scroll through the pages of this book?

- What is your relationship to your self-worth?

- Are you identifying labels from your FOO that no longer resonate with you?

- How did it feel in your body to read about familial and societal standards of worth?

- Do you have an awareness of splitting parts of yourself?

- Do you have any experience with feeling like you were either less than or above other people? How did this dictate how you treated yourself and allowed yourself to be treated?

- How were you treated in your FOO? What did you observe about how others were treated in your family?

- Who was the golden child (the favorite), the black sheep (the troublemaker), the forgotten child (the one who faded away into the background)? If you were an only child maybe you experienced all three of these at different times.

- Who took care of your parents'/primary caretakers' emotional needs? Were their emotional needs outsourced to you or your sibling(s)?

- Was your parent/primary caretaker interested in listening to you, to your thoughts, and to how your day went?

- What did your family value? That might have included sports, education, beauty, secrecy, silence, money, social status, perfection, alcohol, people-pleasing, racism, or any number of things.

- Was one person allowed to lose their temper/express BIG emotions while everyone else got small and remained quiet?

- Did you feel valued? How were you told you were valued either directly or by observable moments?

- Were you allowed to question the status quo?

- Were you smothered? Neglected? Both?

- How did the family handle you when you were upset? Or needy or sad or angry?

- What was happening for you to know when you were being valued? Were gifts involved? Attention?

- Did someone have to be less than you for you to be valued? Was comparison part of your worth equation in the FOO?

- Were you noticed only when you were sick?

- Were you valued when you made good grades or took care of your siblings? When you kept Dad's secrets or stopped Mom from crying? When you won games or performances? When you looked prettier than anyone else? Were you valued for what you could produce for the family or primary caretakers? Were you expected to uphold a certain image?

- Were you allowed to have needs and desires? Did you hold in your beliefs/needs/desires for the ease of the group?

- Were you allowed to rest, or did you have to consistently be in motion?

- Did you feel safe? What did you learn about your body?

- What did you learn about your gender and the roles that gender had in the family system? Were you allowed to talk positively or with curiosity about your body?

Follow your curiosity of your memories/awareness to where they want to take you. After all, there's a lot to unpack. Although it may seem laborious and will certainly make you feel vulnerable, this exploration is a large part of what the process of uncovering your connection to your self-worth is all about—after all, we can't change what we can't see in ourselves. We can't rewrite stories if we aren't aware of the stories in the first place.

It might be helpful to look at this activity from the standpoint of you're gaining data on yourself and taking inventory. You're being curious about your origins so you can gain clarity on what your old stories are for the purpose of unlearning and reprogramming your system. In this context, "your system" is your awareness, your nervous system, your reactions, your energetic authority, your congruence and embodiment, and your relationship to your self-worth.

Nugget

A tool that helps me, when I'm going through old, sticky memories is to remember that I already lived through those experiences. In my current reality, nothing like that is actually happening except I am feeling the sensations associated with the memory. The stories my psyche created about what was happening and why, they no longer have power over me unless I give them power and the feelings can't and won't kill me. The hardest part was living through it and I've done that. Now I get to be the detective and see the old story for what it is and where it keeps cycling in my mind and body.

Likewise, you too can see your memory for what it is: a story of the past, an adaptation that's no longer necessary for your current lifestyle. Feel your feelings around it, give yourself (child, teenage, young person) compassion, and let that part of you know that you are no longer living in that experience. If that feels too hard, just gaining the recognition that you lived through some hard times is all the validation you need to keep going. You can't mess this process up!

Before we go any further, though, I think it's important to recognize that not everyone will identify their FOO as being bad, traumatic, abusive, and/or harmful. I'm not here to say "Yes they were!" and that you're delusional. What I am promoting is for you to be curious about how you were impacted regardless of the intent. We've all seen and heard stories of siblings growing up in the same environment (or two people experiencing the same event) and one is rocked to their core while the other person experiences it like water off a duck's back.

This is not about the FOO's dynamic, necessarily, but rather the impact the dynamic had on you. Your self-identification within the

FOO is what we're looking to uncover. So if you're one of the people who grew up in an ideal household, I'm not about blaming your parents and caretakers, but I am curious about you and what you perceived outside of other's intentions. In some cases, it may have nothing to do with the family—perhaps a traumatic event occurred and that shaped how you see yourself in the world.

One more reflection is one concerning respect. I often hear of people who were undeniably loved by their parents, had resources, had community, etc. but did not know the feeling of respect—of being fully seen, accepted, and held in their autonomy, respected who they were as children as well as into their teenage and adult years. That has an impact ya'll!

So, take a deep breath. Sit with these questions and be curious about what you find. Notice any feelings and reactions that are associated with these memories– is there a quickening in your system or do you feel overwhelmed? Notice, too, if you had no reaction and only felt numb. Remember, everything is a spectrum here– and most often layered– so any and every response is okay and normal.

Based on how much you've looked at these memories of your past, your responses may transform over time. You may find that the more often you visit these questions, the deeper they'll affect you and the more your mind and body will remember. Think of this as mining your lived experiences to reveal where your "stuff" lives in both your mind and body.("Stuff" is your triggers, your sore spots; it's where you get stuck in repeating patterns and seemingly never move past the lesson of the recurring situation.)

Answering these questions may take time. Frankly, I hope they do. You may stay in the emotional soup of identifying experiences and feeling feelings in response to these questions for a period of time. Memories may rise to the surface that are not exact answers to these particular questions but to other questions; other memories may pop up randomly. This is all proof that something within you is moving. The lube of self-inquiry is working.

As memories rise to the surface of your mind, write them down. Slow down long enough to feel yourself (even if it feels like nothing is happening) and take a moment to practice compassion for your younger self. That self didn't deserve these stories/experiences, but your younger self had to acquire them in order to survive the family and/ or societal system. If you have no relationship with your younger self, not to worry– more on that later. And remember, the silver lining is that you survived. Good job! That's your innate intelligence working for you.

Nugget

Move often during this work– go for a walk or take a bath or do whatever feels like a "fuck, YES!" to your body. Let things release and recalibrate. Then rest.

CHAPTER 2

Tools for Identification and Unlearning

Gathering information about your experience thus far has no doubt been an extraordinary process. The unlearning step begins by taking one of those stories that told you that you were (un)worthy in the past and notice how it's showing up in your life today.

Let's work with the example I provided earlier, the one about the middle child who wasn't considered attractive and was always blamed for being unreasonable. We're going to consider some stories held by the family of origin about this kid. The middle child could have been the forgotten child, meaning that the eldest and the youngest got the most attention and the middle child blended into the background... except for when they didn't. Perhaps they acted out, giving them the label of "unreasonable" or "bad." They learned indirectly that they had less value than their siblings because they weren't given the same amount of attention unless they acted out. That resulted in them getting the attention they craved, albeit for the most part negative attention. (A note: while I don't necessarily believe in the reductive polarity of negative and positive or good and bad in terms of human behavior, for simplicity's sake, I believe that using these words illustrates or at least gives you an easily digestible understanding of the example used in the scenario.)

So now we have a child growing up with the belief that they aren't as valuable as others. Attached to their core belief is that they gain attention through negative enactments. As they grow up, they make choices out of that core belief. This person will almost certainly continue to act out in negative ways to gain attention. The negative attention and/or consequences then begin to build "proof" in their mind that they are in fact not good enough. This of course is not actual proof that they're bad and deserve negative attention, but to the unexamined mind, it will certainly appear that way.

This scenario is often at the root of the matter when you hear people (or maybe yourself) say, "If I'm not bad then why do I keep getting all this bad attention? Why do all these bad things keep happening to me? I must be bad." Really what happened was their intelligent mind had to create a story based on the person's need to remain safe in their experience of the past. That same intelligent mind then had to make decisions (again, stemming from historical subconscious beliefs) to continue producing scenarios for them to "prove" to themself that they're bad, unworthy, wrong, broken, or damaged. It's like a snake eating its own tail or like a self-fulfilling prophecy.

Do you relate to this pattern?

In case I haven't said it enough, these stories that are imposed upon us by our FOO and/or by society are bullshit! They are not real. The person from the example is not bad. They never were! They just internalized a story about who they thought they were based on their environment. Identifying these underlying beliefs is critical, because as you move through life, you're making decisions based on these core ideas...which in turn are based on historical stories and evidence (or lack of it).

Another part of this conversation has to do with perception. The perception piece is huge because what you focus on grows. If you think you're bad, choose experiences that strengthen that belief and you'll only notice all the bad in your life. If this is the case for you, I imagine part of your experience is missing pieces. Can you recall memories from your life (perhaps from your childhood) when you felt good about yourself? When you felt the warmth of someone who loved you? Can you recall a time when satisfaction was your primary feeling? Sit in that memory for a moment longer and allow your awareness of the parts of you that feel good to expand.

Nugget

Consider the messages/stories/held beliefs you received from your FOO or society. Are they beliefs that you want to define your worth today? How does it feel in your body when you think about them? How are those old stories showing up in your current life structure? What choices have you made to maintain those beliefs and keep them alive in your life today?

The final question is a responsibility check-in for yourself. Part of change is taking what has been unconscious and making it conscious, which I believe you are doing by reading this book. The second part of your responsibility is to do the work within this book: answer the questions, live through the sensations, and gain clarity on what you find. The third part is to take responsibility for the information you've gained and begin to transform your life. What I mean by "transform" is to look at what has been, for the purposes of clearing those stories, create what resonates with you now, and then begin living with your new awareness. I'll expand on self-responsibility more in later chapters.

If you are at the point where the stories you've uncovered no longer resonate, you may notice you are feeling a certain kinda way– possibly anger, grief, confusion, disbelief, and even a sense of powerlessness are bubbling into your awareness. Good! Feel those feelings! Know that they are yours and that you will be responsible for them. How can you take a moment to express your harder truths and feelings in a supportive way? Could you cry, scream, shred some paper? Do you feel called to write a letter to your FOO/society/ex-lover/high school P.E. teacher that you have no intention of sending? Do Not Send this letter! But do write it for the cathartic practice of getting your thoughts out of your mind and onto paper. (You can burn that shit later on.) Would it be supportive to tell your therapist or a close confidant about your truths and feelings? Would moving your body help to sort things out?

This is such an important part of the process! I can not stress that enough. Your feelings are valid. You might not even know what you're feeling. You may not have a name for the sensation—you just know something is moving, something feels heavy, something feels like a chokehold on your throat or a pit in your stomach. Bring your awareness to your body. Acknowledge and breathe into any places where you're sensing any kind of energy.

Breathe.

Once you've allowed yourself to feel all the things and once you've cleared some space within you and rested and hydrated, get curious about what life could look like and feel like with a different belief about yourself. Have you ever allowed yourself to even consider that there is another story, another belief is possible for you? What would you like to believe differently about yourself right now? Can you admit to yourself that you are not what they said but are in fact something else– something better, more aligned, someone who gets to decide for themselves?

That final question in particular begs for you to step into more of your own power, so go back and read it again. You may feel ready for the embodiment of your own power or you may not in this exact moment, but know that your power is a big part of this conversation. Your sense of power and your self-sovereignty to choose for yourself who you are and what you believe about yourself at any given moment is always present, whether you're attuned to it or not. I empower you to begin stepping into and embodying your power. It is safe and it is necessary.

Nugget

This is where you pause and write on a Post-it note: "It is safe to change. I release the idea that I am not enough." On another write: "It is safe to change and I am willing to see myself differently."

FOO and Friends

Around this time in the process, my clients are typically flooded with thoughts of family, friends, and people with whom they have close interpersonal relationships (including work colleagues and associates of all kinds and communities) showing up in their psyche to say, "No, don't go there! You can't change, because that would mean you would disappoint me/us. I will leave you. I will be upset by you changing, and your [verbal or nonverbal] agreement is to maintain the status quo!"

It's important to recognize the places in your mind where you get hooked into a pattern. After all, you may be right– your family/friends may indeed respond in exactly the manner you anticipate. Why would they do that? Perhaps they don't know any better. They aren't on the same journey of self-awareness that you are; maybe they don't want to see you grow. They don't know that change is possible for them. They are scared. No matter why they respond the way they respond, though, you need to realize that this is the established relationship pattern.

If you no longer wish to be in that pattern, once you've realized it's there, know that change is on your horizon. Notice how maintaining the status quo within the relationship– remaining silent, staying small, ignoring your needs/desires–serves you or doesn't serve you. Ask yourself, "Does this relationship support me acting from a place of clarity and alignment with my self-worth?" What tools would you need to develop or strengthen to feel safe enough to change while maintaining these relationships? Where is your alignment to yourself within the relationship? Is your preference towards growth or to the maintenance of remaining the same for the comfort of another?

Inner Parts

Take a deep breath! It's time to access your courage. To do that, we're going to go full woo-woo. You're going to deliberately take a look into and sense parts of yourself that may not get lots of attention in your normal day-to-day life. (I'm applauding your courageousness right now!)

Take a moment to get quiet; settle into your body and open up to the awareness of your inner world below your neck. By that, I mean stop thinking your thinky thoughts. Get out of your head and start feeling into your body. Where are the old stories living within you (i.e. "I'm not good enough," "I'm bad," "I'll never be smart enough," "I need others to like me in order for me to validate myself") and what do they feel like? Where are you storing them–your guts, your shoulders, your jaw? What does it feel like? Pressure? Barbed wire? Rocks? A black hole?

Try to breathe into those spaces. Expand your awareness of them and get curious about what else is there, if anything. Trust what you find even if it feels scary, stupid, silly, illogical, or totally out of left field. Notice the space these sensations occupy. Can you begin to notice that the sensation is within you but not of you? Meaning, can you notice it, sense into it, feel it, give it a name, and realize it's an energetic space in your body but also that it's not you? The voices that tell you "I'm bad" are internalized voices that are not yours.

Try to feel what age you were when this sensation began to take shape in your body. It may take persistent curiosity to recognize and identify these sensations inside of you. The point is not to stay with the sensation long enough to retraumatize yourself– rather, you want to be curious of where and how you've been holding this energetic and emotional block/trauma/energy in your body. By giving it physical attributes, you can begin to identify how much energetic weight you've been carrying and how much of your history is taking up space in your current life and body. You also get an externalized perception of this energy. Again, it's not actually you– most likely, it was created at some point for the purposes of protection. But now you don't need that protection anymore. You can explore your inner world! It's finally okay to sense and feel into the shadows. Deep breath...

To further examine what I'm saying, let's go with an example of guilt (big sigh!). You've sensed into your body and have noticed tension in your shoulders, and when you get curious about the tension, an awareness of guilt shows up. You don't know why, exactly– it's just an intuitive hit of guilt. Trust that. Your brain may try to rationalize it, but don't! Just go with it. Allow your awareness to extend beyond the proof of rationale.

The tension feels like a bag of rocks you've been carrying on your shoulders, a weight created by guilt. It's very heavy, dense, and monotonous. Although the story of "I'm Bad" no longer resonates, the guilt of removing that idea and living from a new thought still feels like a giant bag of rocks on your shoulders. (Stay with me here...) The rocks tell you that you have to maintain living and thinking this way about yourself.

That's a beautiful awareness! Keep going. Notice if you can remove some of the rocks (because this is your imagination after all). With this awareness, do you want to maintain the bag of rocks or would you like another option? If it were me, I would want to get rid of that bag of rocks. Would it feel good to set them down? Maybe throw them down or have water sweep them away forever?

I share this example to show you that you can gain an understanding that the rocks don't have to hold the same power over you that they once did. You can begin to interact with these parts of your psyche and gain a new relationship with them. You can feel a new sense of urgency and overcome the guilt and finally put that shit down. You can address any stories about yourself and potentially let some of them go in order to "lighten your load," so to speak.

Combining the "I'm bad" sensation of heaviness with an externalized idea of rocks allows you to powerfully move out of old realities and into new ones that will ultimately benefit your self-concept. This process promotes stepping into your power.

Nugget

Now move your body. Literally, move as if you're taking a load of rocks off your back. (Phew!) Take a breath. Maybe cry a little and allow your body to shake. (Shaking indicates an energetic and nervous system release and the recalibration of your cells.) Reach into your bag and grab a rock– it could be a rolled-up ball of paper or a ball of socks or just your imagination. How would it feel to throw that rock? To throw it at the wall or into your backyard? How would it feel to brush it vigorously away from you or perhaps simply set it down? However your intuition wants to handle this moment is right—just invite action into your process, an action that allows your body and your subconscious to recognize that something is shifting and you are no longer willing to carry "it" anymore. This is BIG. Continue to be open and observe what's happening inside you.

Breathe, burn some sage, and rest. Revisit this at any time.

Notice if a part of you is relieved to finally stop and look at the thing you typically run away from or avoid looking at or carrying around like it's no big deal. Notice how courageous that part of you is for pausing long enough to simply just look and be curious.

Validation of Your Inner Parts

You are a multidimensional being with many parts alive within you. You know this because you can sit and follow your mind into fantasyland, creating worlds and interacting with thoughts from your past and future scenes. You can think of all kinds of things, places, people, and experiences that aren't in your current 3D reality. That's your multidimensional capability impacting your emotional body into responding, like remembering a funny scene in a movie and laughing about it after the fact or thinking of a person you find attractive and feeling your body get turned on. Or daydreaming about telling someone off and feeling righteous anger swell in your face...the list of possibilities goes on and on.

Recognize your power of creation! You can also experience multiple responses at once– think about getting pissed at having to get off the highway to refuel your car because you know you'll be late getting to work and feeling happy because you know your tardiness will mean you'll juuuuuust miss seeing your annoying boss during the shift change. A pissed part and a happy part can live simultaneously in your awareness.

How all of this relates to self-worth is knowing that yes, there are parts of you that want to throw you off the path to accepting that you're worthy... and parts of you that are desperate to know and believe that you're worthy. Both are happening simultaneously. By identifying them, you'll have a better chance of working with them to know what they did and did not receive/do and do not receive with regard to accepting your entire being. By giving yourself and your parts the loving attention and emotional validation that your parts did not receive—and doing so with genuine curiosity—you can build an awareness of when they learned to hide or contort themselves into believing stories that maintained your sense of unworthiness. In doing this, you get to give your parts what they needed. You get to perform the act of re-parenting, healing those parts, and moving them into a supportive self-awareness.

It's important to continue noticing and validating the many parts of you, the layers of this experience, and this feeling. Know that each of these parts has wisdom and validity. That's true for both the ones that want to stay small and the ones that are ready for growth. It's true for the parts that are holding the old stories in place and the parts that want something new; the parts that aren't sure, the parts that are afraid, the parts that tell you this process is stupid and not worth it— they tell you that perhaps that you are stupid and not worth it and not capable. The parts of you that are ready to get on with it and the parts that would prefer to sit down and watch TV and forget any of this ever happened. The parts that say you can't change because Mom and Dad and your partner and your kids and your boss and your neighbor and on and on and on are not going to handle this well. (This is a great way to identify who you give your power away to!)

*Pro-tip: Other people's emotions are not your responsibility. It is not your responsibility to handle them nor soothe their upset. You have a choice. And frankly, so do they. Perhaps your growth will inspire theirs! Respect yourself and respect their process enough to let go of managing it all. Their needs don't have to be yours. Let go! They will be okay without you doing all of the work for them. Even if they cannot recognize that truth right now.

CHAPTER 3

Parts Work/Inner Child/ Teenager

Developing a sense of and relationship with your inner child and inner teenager can have a profound impact on the process of healing. It was during these times that you consciously or subconsciously cut off (inner) parts of yourself, affecting your connection to your self-worth in order to survive within your established FOO/environment. Reclaiming these younger parts often produces a new relationship with and alignment with yourself in a whole-body, entire-life kinda way. It embodies a fresh understanding of who you are in any situation because you're no longer cut off and hiding parts of yourself. This is power! It's the power of knowing yourself and an ease to your knowingness because there's nothing to hide and nothing to lose.

Nugget

Create time to sit undisturbed. Close your eyes and turn your focus inward. Get grounded through your breath; be aware of the weight of your body and the depth of your breath.

Call forth a younger version of yourself. Recall a time in your childhood or teenage years when you received the message you were "not enough." Allow yourself to go back in your mind and slow that scene down. Notice the details—but don't let them distract you!---and truly feel the feelings. Really be there in that memory. What was happening from your perspective? Only your perspective is important here. Who was there? What was the message and How old were you?

Enter the memory as the adult self you are today and sit with your younger self. Introduce yourself as the older and wiser version of yourself. Let them know you mean no harm—rather, you want to protect them and get to know them. You want to witness, feel, and validate their feelings.

How would it feel to remove your younger self from the perceived scenario to a safer place? If that doesn't feel natural or necessary, find a way to create safety right where they/you are. Connect with them: look into their eyes, hold their hand, and sit close to them. Let the background fade away. Tell them you are here now. Tell them, "This event was inappropriate/scary/no bueno and you didn't and don't deserve that treatment. You are worth far more love, attention, patience, respect, understanding, and compassion than that moment carried for you."

Make sure they know in their deepest of hearts that the message conveyed in the memory is not their fault. They no longer have to live with the idea that they're somehow not worthy or enough. Ask what you can give them– how you can be of service? How could you reclaim their safety/self-worth/power/sovereignty for them? Sit with this question, it is important.

Let them rest in your presence. In this moment give them what was missing for them in the past experience. This is where your multidimensional powers get to create a scene where your inner child receives everything they needed. Guess what? Your brain doesn't know the difference. This is the magic elixir of healing your parts! Your brain is telling a new story, but this time it's one that actually serves you. Could the parts of you that keep you focused on logic and being "right" soften just a little right now? Soften just enough for the healing you are trying to create for yourself and your younger ones to have impact? Would it be ok, if just for this moment, you could rely on imagination rather than impermeable walls of logic? You could release trying to control and instead be open to the possibility of connection with yourself.

If connecting with the younger part of yourself doesn't seem to come easily, know that sometimes being patient with this vulnerable part is necessary. The younger parts of ourselves can respond with enthusiasm, like "Thank god you're here—now I can do the business of being a child," but other times, it may take time to make a connection with the younger versions of ourselves, particularly if we've been used to pushing them aside for years, keeping them in the shadows and compartmentalizing them in boxes hidden far away within the psyche. You may feel resistance to this part of the work; they may be angry at you for denying their existence. If you've been angry at this younger part, if you've been telling it hurtful things, or if you've been ashamed of it for years, consider that it may take time to develop the relationship to a place of openness and trust.

If you're not easily able to connect to your younger inner parts but you desire to lean in and grow that connection– or even if you would like to acquire a sense of connection for the sake of nurturing your younger self outside of trauma healing–consider ways that you could appeal to them.

One of those ways could be journaling about the younger part of yourself that you would like to connect with now. How old is the younger part of yourself you'd like to connect with now? Do you recall things you liked to do at that age? Or things you never got to do but always wanted to? What did you like to eat? What was your favorite movie, color, game, activity? Perhaps you would be open to writing a letter to your younger self. Think about what you would say. Do you have a picture of yourself at that age? If you do, think about what it would be like to put that picture in a place where you'd see it every day. I once saw a reel that RuPaul posted about this exact thing—he made a picture of his 5-year-old self as his phone's screen saver. So cute!

Once you've identified what lights up your younger self, take time to be with them. You know what they like, so how could you incorporate that food and those activities into your present day? Let's say it's coloring or riding a bike. Could you do that now? Or maybe you could listen to the music you liked as a child. For me, that's The Little Mermaid soundtrack, although, as a teenager, it was more like 90's grunge bands. Totally different vibes, right?

Getting a sense of the age of your younger self is important, so know what tools you can use to access the various stages of your life. Start to incorporate these things as much or as often as you'd like with the intent of creating joy and connection with that part of yourself. This part of you is tender (and maybe angsty), so try to connect in a way that promotes tenderness. If you're only accessing your inner child to access the hard and heavy parts and heal past traumas then how will the relationship have an opportunity to blossom?

Who's Responding?

How to know when you're responding from your inner child or teenager takes a keen sense of awareness built from introspection. The introspection can be gained by answering the questions in this book and developing your relationship with your younger self. To use an example from my own life, I notice when I'm responding from my inner teenager to a person or experience because the reaction will have a lot more attitude. My tone will usually be accompanied by an eye-roll and defensive/fuck-it mentality. I'll know it's my wounded child reacting when I feel like someone might be judging me and I want to get small or if I believe my voice is not perceived as valid or important or if I impishly wonder if I'm good enough.

Notice your response versus reaction to life and the people around you. This noticing allows you to build self-awareness and gauge what part of you is responding. Are you in control of your response, or are you just kinda along for the ride alongside whatever is flying out of your mouth at the moment? Do your responses feel more extreme than what the current moment is asking for? In other words, consider whether your reaction/response has a historically charged energy. That usually occurs because a wounded part of you and/or resentments are piling up. The energy you've been trying to hold back by not being honest with yourself (or perhaps you're unaware of an issue) and having to instead address things as they come up is now bubbling over and making your reactions strong and emotional. No worries. This happens to the best of us.

Another way to determine what part of you is responding is to gain a clear sense of your "higher self" and how that part responds to life. Your higher self is the part of you that responds with integrity, dignity, grace, and wisdom: maybe it's your ideal you. If you have no idea about this part of yourself, then now is a good time to begin developing an awareness of it. How does your higher self/evolved self/wisdom mind (whatever you want to call it) respond, speak, stand, and be in relationship to the world around them? The embodied feeling of this part of yourself versus the angry teenager or the scared child is totally different. It's like being sad rather than happy or full versus hungry—the feeling is way different.

CHAPTER 4

Guilt and Shame

Looking at guilt and shame are often the heaviest parts of our journey as we unlearn, relearn, and heal parts of ourselves. (The energy of guilt and shame is thick and it's hella dense.) That's in part why this process is often referred to and feels like "work"---you're moving out of one system, one patterned way of being, and transforming into another. Oftentimes there's a price to pay for doing this work: the price of change. That often looks and often feels like a death of your old/ habituated way of being, including relationships with people, places, and things that color your world... including people, places, and things that at some point may have felt like love, joy and connection.

Sigh.

Consider unlearning and rebuilding your connection to your self-worth as being like seismic shifts in the Earth's layers. They feel monumental because they are! If you're on a fault line, you'll feel some earthquakes as things shake up and get disrupted. Sometimes there's even death. How can you embrace death while also planting the seeds for something new to be born?

I urge you to be kind and gentle towards yourself during this process. Remind yourself that any discomfort you might feel as you grow your self-worth will be temporary. It will not be this painful forever! These feelings are TEMPORARY. Yes, death is hard and it hurts—there's grief and sometimes part of the process will make you feel pissed off. Pissed that you're the one having to change and grow and that you're the one blessed with changing the family dynamics. On top of that, you have to leave your usual coping tools behind because they're not really working anymore anyway. The cherry on the top is you thinking, "What about everyone else? Do they just get to continue in ignorance? Why do I have to do all this work to be happy?" Maybe for a brief period, you do, and maybe they won't ever understand you, but other people aren't really your concern right now. The focus is on being really sweet and patient with yourself as you figure out this part of your journey. Trust me, it gets way more fulfilling as you gain the momentum of your own alignment!

I also want to introduce the concept of growing in joy here too. The work does not always have to feel heavy– hold the possibility of being able to transform with ease, grace, and even joy. Like maybe you think, "Thank God, I don't have to do this shit anymore! Next please!" A lot of people (myself included at times) don't listen to the "quiet whispers" as Oprah calls them. Those are your intuitions knocking at the door of your awareness, saying, "Something is wrong!" or "Don't date that person" or "Take your time making this decision."

Be aware of when your mind goes into overdrive and plows right over that quiet whisper, thinking, "It'll be okay. I can handle it— they'll change." Maybe, but maybe not. Are you willing to face whatever consequences maybe? What is your intention? Have you faced the same or a very similar situation before and ended up licking your wounds because surprise, they didn't change? I know I have!

Compassion is essential for the part of you that made you override all the quiet whispers and sometimes led to having yelling matches between your head and heart. What if you could try trusting yourself? Maybe the quiet whisper is actually your intuition, your gut-brain communicating to you. Maybe you can override the people-pleaser part of your habitual behavior telling you to move forward with an experience that on some level you know will eventually hurt you more than them. Do you have a week, a month, or ten years to figure out how to speak your truth? Could you stop and breathe and then choose yourself? Bypassing the potentially-years-long relationship of turmoil and instead disappointing them right now? Ultimately setting yourself (and them) free.

The truth is that the quiet whisper or intuition is your self-preservation. This is the self-respect and the self-love that you're looking for in an outside person, place, or thing. Believe me, whether the other person wants a relationship, money, and/or attention from you, they'll find it in someone else who's willing to take what you're no longer available to take on.

Nugget

Repeat after me: "I can learn in a state of ease. I can unlearn and relearn, release, and recalibrate in ways that are gentle for my nervous system."

Can you recognize the guilt and shame that have kept your old stories of unworthiness in place? Your survival wiring kept them in place to keep you stuck (and at some point, safe) in the system. That undoubtedly worked for a period of time. But building self-worth—although scary and intense at times—will ultimately get you out of the scarcity mindset of thinking "I'm not valuable unless I do or believe in these ways" into "I have value and an unshakeable knowing of my worth."

What are the stories that guilt and shame tell you? How are they devaluing your right to exist? They might even be devaluing your desire to want anything better/different/more aligned—they might be telling you that anything different or better is not possible for you. Maybe they are saying that you did something wrong and now you must suffer (forever) repeatedly, or that if you changed and sought another way for yourself, you'd be abandoning others. Guilt and/or shame often say, "You can't because of X" or "You just aren't worth it, so there's no use in trying?" or That works for others, but not for you—your brokenness is too deep."

Explore these messages. Look them square in the eyes and follow where they lead. Then question them and their validity. Look for the "proof" that you can't change. Question if you need to hold on to the guilt anymore and get curious about how it could shift. Think about what within you would need to change in order to make that shift. Is something just a belief that others have imposed upon you? Do you need to forgive yourself or another? Are the guilt and shame even yours, or are you holding onto someone else's belief for/of you? Consider how you would prepare to believe something different. From my own story, I have internalized messages that "I'm all to blame and it's all my fault." Through this work, I realized that it is internalized guilt and shame that resulted from being raised by parents that wouldn't take responsibility for themselves and blamed me instead. As an adult that ultimately resulted in me being in relationships with people who didn't take responsibility and I would think I was the reason they didn't love, respect, and value me because I wasn't X enough.

Visualize and feel what this process of transforming/healing/forgiving/letting go of guilt and shame could look and feel like for you. Imagine what you would look like, stand like, breathe like, and speak like if you were to transform the guilt and shame into radical self-acceptance. Think about how your outlook would change if forgiveness were a part of your journey. Remember, you're also facing the forgiveness of yourself. Releasing the idea of "I am not worthy" opens the possibility of "I am worthy" and that creates space for [fill in your desires here].

Journal about all of your findings. Or draw or sketch out or paint whatever this process looks like for you.

A note on forgiving: please do not rush this process. Take your time. Your complete honesty is necessary here. If you're angry or hurt or sad, please take all the time you need to feel these feelings for as long as you need to. My personal reflection is that there's a movement in the spiritual community to forgive and move on as a means of spiritual bypassing, of moving on to get to the other side of living your best Instagram life in photos for all to see without working through the process of feeling deep feelings. This is bullshit! It's not real and it's disrespectful to yourself. (Parent moment: why do we force kids to apologize and make up so quickly? To act like everything is okay and just move on? It's totally disrespectful and oftentimes not an effective tool for learning or forgiving.)

Take your time. Respect yourself and your journey and the parts of you that need validation. You'll know when the process feels complete, trust me. Only then begin to look beyond the veil and rise from the ashes, however, this feeling of readiness emerges for you. Ask yourself what you're willing to release in order to see this person and/or event differently. What did you learn? And how would you like to move forward?

CHAPTER 5

Boundaries

Boundaries create a sense of safety and a sort of organizational framework as to what you're available for in terms of people, places, and things. When people grow up in family systems that are codependent and/or unsupportive of each individual's needs, boundaries feel elusive, strange, and wrong, but boundaries are honestly a means of letting others know where you stand. They create safety and clarity and are a significant means of support for you. It's ok to have boundaries! In fact, all healthy relationships have them. Even unhealthy relationships have boundaries, although in those cases, the boundaries usually support one person while sucking the life out of the other(s).

Consider boundaries to be a support structure for you, made by you in support of you. Boundaries provide guidance for others to let them know what you're available for in a relationship. Boundaries are self-care in motion. Lets go over three types of boundaries:

The wall. This boundary is like an impenetrable wall: nothing is getting through. This sounds something like "I never wish to speak to you again." And then you don't speak to them ever again.

No boundary. When there is no boundary in sight, that can sound like "Call anytime! No problem– I'll always pick up no matter what." And then you do pick up at any time, no matter what.

Malleable boundaries. These are most often used in interpersonal relationships. They can change as needed within the relationship: "Do not call me during business hours unless you text me first and I say it's okay to call me."

Boundaries are necessary in all areas of your life. The following list will help you recognize where you are and are not allowing boundaries to support you. Note the areas where you feel confident setting boundaries and the areas where you don't. And feel free to add to the list for yourself:

Physical Boundaries
- You get to determine the quality and quantity of your food yourself.
- You get to choose when, where, and how often you take your rest.
- You get to claim your personal space, and if someone is too close for comfort, you get to say so.

Emotional Boundaries
- You get to determine what you share about yourself when and

with whom.

- You get to determine your emotional capacity for any person, place, or thing.

- You get to decide if you want to receive support from someone regardless of how that will affect them.

Time

- You get to claim time for yourself.

- You get to manage your work life, family, friendships, extracurricular activities, etc.

- You get to go at a speed that feels in alignment for you.

Sexual

- You get to decide whom you have sex with and receive any sexually charged touch from.

- You get to make decisions about contraception.

- You get to name your boundaries around frequency, when, and where.

Intellectual

- You get to choose to spend time with people and share your ideas where they will be respected.

- You get to decide if you are open for debates.

- You get to determine if you want to educate yourself.

Material

- You get to decide if you want to share your money,

- You get to decide if you want to receive money from people and organizations.

- You get a say in how your material possessions are treated.

Spiritual/Religious

- You get to choose if you worship and where.

- You get to choose your religious beliefs and affiliations.

Political

- You get to decide whom you politically align with and support.

- You never have to defend or explain your choices.

Where in your life do you have boundaries that feel supportive? Are you great at setting boundaries at work but struggle to set them with your friends or partner? Do you have boundaries with money but not with food? Think about where your boundaries work for you and where you have none. Consider where your boundaries are rigid or flexible. Also, consider what it's like to create boundaries. Were boundaries allowed in your FOO? Equally important—perhaps even more so—do you believe you're worth protecting? Perhaps you find it easy to create a boundary but hard to maintain it, or maybe you quickly cut others out without ever sharing your boundaries with them. Do you know you're allowed to say yes one day and no the very next? Examine whether or not conversations about boundaries feel comfortable for you. What would it feel like to say, "I am no longer available for X?"

Unfortunately, many people have grown up in a family where self-worth was not taught and not valued. If that was you, you're probably prone to putting up walls or not having any boundaries at all. Let's look at how those scenarios of not promoting self-worth show up in family systems.

Maybe your brother was allowed to do anything he wanted: staying out late, yelling at you, stealing money from Mom's purse with no consequences. Meanwhile, you only got attention when you were sick and were expected to clean the house. Oftentimes, your mother would baby you even though you asked her not to. You were forced to hug your creepy family member even though you protested. You were told as a child that children are to be seen and not heard and what did children know, anyway? (That last one was definitely a message I heard over and over again growing up.) You were forced to only eat a limited amount of calories so you'd always appear slim. Your parents could go through your things at any time because you were living under their roof, they told you. (Me again.) You were not allowed to sit down and rest– you had to always appear busy, or else you would be called lazy. Doors were never allowed to be closed for privacy and you were never allowed to share your opinions.

The list goes on and on. Those examples display a clear lack of supportive boundaries that would have created a safe space to grow in and learn from. But whether your FOO treated you that way or they didn't, in order to grow your sense of self-worth now, you need boundaries with others and with yourself. That means no more mindlessly bad-mouthing yourself anymore.

Noticing how you feel around others is going to play a huge part in understanding what your needs and wants are. Get clear on what you want to support in your life—only then will you begin to understand where your boundaries need to be placed. An example of setting boundaries could be that you'd like more privacy in your life when it comes to your mother. You want to support your own desires to have a healthy level of physical, emotional, and intellectual detachment from her while remaining in a relationship with her. When you're with her, you notice when you're getting activated (annoyed, angry, short-tempered) by her presence.

For instance, say you gave your mom your house key for "emergencies," but she seems to just pop in whenever she likes. You notice that when she experiences anything upsetting in her day, she calls you first to tell you every detail without ever pausing to ask you if you have the time and emotional capacity for her at that moment. When you tell her about any new idea or concept you're considering trying out, and she tells you all the ways it won't work for you.

In all of these examples, you play a part. Therefore, you have a responsibility to yourself to create a new support structure that could support you staying in a relationship with your mother and having the space you need to be your own sovereign being/adult.

I can hear you saying, "Ha! But you don't know my mother!" And you're right—I don't! What I do know is that creating boundaries with this woman will take some courage on your part, and it will also take consistency. After all, she may not even know that these things are bothering you because you've never mentioned them to her in the first place. (I like to lead with the benefit of the doubt.) Maybe she just truly did not know, and after you've told her your boundaries, you'll both be illuminated by the power of your voice and her appreciation for you trusting her with your truth.

Of course, the more challenging option is that she does know that these things bother you but doesn't have the capacity to care about your needs. Also (and probably very likely), she doesn't care about your needs above her own. If that's the case, you're still allowed to have needs and speak them into existence. You do not have to care-take her disappointment. Trust that if she does not handle your boundaries well, she's responding from a wounded part. It's not your responsibility to heal her. The truth is, you can't do her "work" for her anyway. If she tries to use guilt and shame to manipulate you, you have a choice there, too: to see it for what it is—an attempt to control you and her wounded parts—or do what you've always done and thus thwart your own growth of separation. What do you want to see and how do you want to proceed?

This is when clients tell me, "I want my mom to know my boundaries without me having to tell her about them." If that's you, you have a fear of stepping into your power and you want to be in relationships with mind readers. Good luck! If your mother isn't a mind reader by now, there's a high likelihood she won't turn into one.

Identify how staying silent is serving you. What within you would need to change and/or be supported to name the boundaries that would support your life and the kind of relationship with your mother that would actually work for you? (And not for the holographic image of you that you've created to keep the peace—that actually is not peaceful for you at all.)

It's worth knowing that you can also change your boundaries at any time without having to explain yourself, that is unless you want to. Your boundaries are yours! Read that again. It is your birthright to define how you want to be treated. It is also your responsibility to be open to hearing about and respecting the boundaries of others. Sometimes discussions are necessary. Sometimes compromise is possible;

sometimes it's not. You get to decide. Also, you get to decide when "No" is a complete sentence.

I hope that this process feels empowering to you. This part of the conversation also touches on your sense of responsibility. What's your connection to the word "responsibility"? Could you create a responsibility to and for yourself to protect yourself? Even if that feels like new territory, try it. Maybe the idea of creating responsibility for and from yourself stirs curiosity within you, or maybe it evokes dread. Think about where you can take more responsibility for yourself with boundaries.

One more point about boundaries: some people decide to cut off their FOO because the toxicity/lack of boundaries is too great of a burden to live with. This decision typically comes after or before learning about and sharing their boundaries, growing their self-worth, attending therapy, doing inner child work, looking at their parts, and trying to find another way.

Sometimes people find that some family members will not or are not available to shift into a healthier way of relating, a way that works for them. If you're experiencing this scenario yet you still desire a relationship with your family, there's an effective method called the "grey rock" method. It was coined by mental health blogger Skylar in 2012. It's when you deliberately act unresponsive or unengaged so that the abusive person will eventually lose interest in you. Essentially, toxic and abusive people thrive on drama, and if you have family members who are often looking for ways to hook you into their drama, they know your "buttons." They know how to get you riled up, try grey rocking them. But by flipping the script on them and not reacting or barely responding if at all, they'll eventually lose interest in you and look for drama elsewhere.

An example of where you could use this technique is if you wanted to stay in a relationship with your younger siblings but still have to navigate Mom and Dad's drama. You can gray-rock Mom and Dad while still having access to the family home and seeing your siblings for family gatherings. Or if you've left an abusive relationship and have children with your ex, try grey rocking your ex so that you can quickly move away from them and get to your kiddo(s) with less drama.

New Vocabulary

Now that you've given yourself permission to feel where you would like to create some boundaries, what kind of boundaries you'd like to create, and with whom you'd like to create boundaries, the second part of this process is the art of saying what you mean and meaning what you say. It can take some time to develop the finesse of articulating where you are and what you need without getting all choked up or avoiding the topic. I like to relate this to much like a pendulum swinging—once the pendulum is on the far left (no boundaries), then it swings to the far right (putting up walls or emotionally charged boundary-setting with lots of anger and tears.) Note that big emotional responses are usually a sign of something historical being triggered, especially if the emotional response does not seem to fit the experience at hand.

Eventually, the pendulum finds a softer swing and lands somewhere in the middle. That's usually where we find our answer. That also points towards nervous system regulation and developing a trust within yourself, a trust that you can and will protect yourself at any cost.

A good way to practice setting boundaries is to notice where it feels safe to do so. Start there: first identify a friend, a family member, or a coworker whom you feel safe with, someone who gives you a green light and you can proceed to share vulnerable parts of yourself. Be curious about their openness to you as well. Practice and develop what it feels like to create a new boundary with your identified safe person. This process will begin to show you three crucial things:

1. You can set boundaries and are capable of setting boundaries.

2. There are people with whom you can set boundaries who will still love/like and accept you.

3. You can grow your capacity to eventually create some larger, more scary boundaries you wish to have in place.

If for whatever reason you do feel fear during this process, remember that you're practicing something new. Sometimes new things don't always feel like you're flowing—instead, they feel like fear, anxiety, or nervous tension. Another nugget to keep in mind is that if setting your boundary with another person didn't go over well or it was totally awkward and you had an out-of-body experience, you do have the ability to create repair with them and with yourself and try again. Repair is essential in any relationship because let's be honest: we are inevitably going to let someone down or upset them at some point. If it's a safe relationship, you can always course-correct and let the other person know you are learning how to create boundaries and you are working on how to communicate them. Thank them for their grace with you while you learn this new skill, and good job for making the effort to create something new for yourself! Perfection is not the goal—the goal is naming your needs in an embodied, present, intentional way so that you can live in relationships in an embodied, present, intentional way.

Visualize yourself creating a boundary with someone you would consider difficult. Notice what body sensations arise for you during the visualization. Can you breathe into those places where the uncomfortable sensation(s) arose? What parts of you need grounding or containment? What stories arose from guilt and shame or powerlessness around setting boundaries? Notice where your desire to create this boundary is coming from. Notice the parts of you that feel ready and the parts of you that aren't quite there yet. Decipher which parts you'll be protecting and clarifying. Notice where there's a possibility for you to soothe the fear and create support for yourself. Are you willing to face any and all possible internal and external consequences of doing so? ("Internal" being your feelings, emotions, and integrity and "external" being the external objective results.) Are the consequences even your responsibility?

Breathe. Visualize creating your boundary and getting the results you want. How does that feel?

Another useful tool is writing out your boundary in your journal before saying or sending it. Get clarity on what you would like to say; explore the vibration and energy you want to be carrying when you share your boundary. Practice saying it in a mirror to yourself. Share it with a trusted individual. (How about your dog?) This will help you to get more clarity and it will be an opportunity for you to practice your words. Once you've created an experience in saying these words, you can lean into your knowingness or lived experience of practicing when the time comes to share your boundary.

Final point: practice making "I" statements. This is not about them—it's about you informing them through your words what the new standard for interacting with you is. Remember, you don't have to explain or clarify your boundary.

CHAPTER 6

Nervous System Regulation and Maintenance

Nervous system regulation is everything. But how can you regulate your system if you've never had experience with doing so? What if your awareness of your nervous system is that you're more often than not in an anxious or fearful state?

In this chapter, I'll give you basic tools for and how to become aware of and regulate your system. I also urge you to speak with a trusted healer who knows about nervous system regulation so that you can engage in one-on-one conversations about taking a customized approach to your body and where you are at this point in your life. Of course, I realize that not everyone has access to a personal healer or therapist. If you do not, check YouTube or wherever you listen to podcasts to find good resources for tools and tips on how to get into your body and regulate your nervous system. (Search for "nervous system regulation.")

Let's start from the beginning: first, how do I know when you're dysregulated? Perhaps your breathing stops, your body tightens, and it's super hard to remain present and in your body (i.e., you disassociate). Or maybe you have a huge emotional response that feels out of control, like extreme sadness or anxiety, and your shame spirals out of control, giving you an overwhelming desire to grab onto a coping/numbing tool. Perhaps you feel compelled to self-harm and/or act impulsively. Do you notice this happening regularly? Perhaps it happens when certain people are around—it might be a part of a pattern of relating to another person.

Here are my top three instant ways to practice nervous system regulation:

1. **Engage in physical and sensorial stimuli.** Take a deep breath. Slow down enough to notice three colors in your immediate space. Name them to yourself. Feel your toes on the ground or in their shoes. Wriggle your toes. Notice what you can hear. Notice what you can taste. What do you smell right now? Rub your hands together gently, building friction between your palms. Rub your thighs. Hummm and feel vibration in the back of your throat. Feel yourself back into the present moment.

2. **If you can, get on the ground.** I mean it. Lay down on the ground and literally get grounded. Grab a pillow to pull onto your chest or over your pelvis and pull a blanket over your body. Get low and get warm. Maybe roll around too. Roll on to your tummy and roll up and down your spine. Explore if that feels like it's bringing you into the present moment.

3. **Dance.** Or if that feels like too much, gently sway. Put some music on, too. Choose whatever music that feels like support for you at this moment.

The purpose of this practice is to gain control over your nervous system, because in order to change, you need to be able to regulate and calm yourself on both a physical and an emotional level. Our ancient ancestors were always on the lookout for danger—think about saber-toothed tigers lying in wait and ready to pounce at any moment. While nowadays we don't have to worry about tigers pouncing on us, our nervous systems are still on alert for potential harm. Know that survival wiring is the strongest wiring we have in our bodies. It will override everything else.

In terms of system regulation, your brain identifies that if you can rub your hands on your thighs or lay on the ground, then you clearly are okay enough to take in what's happening in the current moment. You get to move through fight, flight, freeze, and fawn– all nervous system responses that occur when the brain perceives danger– and move into a place of regulation and ultimately control.

Let me break this down for you with an example. Say you're worried about talking to your boss about a promotion you've been wanting. You know you're worthy of it (because you certainly are!) but every time you consider having the conversation, you begin to sweat, you feel jittery in your stomach, your heart rate quickens, and you can barely feel your feet on the ground. Those are all the signs that your nervous system is hijacking your body. To avoid these feelings, you avoid having the conversation even though you know in your heart of hearts that it's time to move forward in your career.

My suggestion would be that while you're alone, sit in a comfortable spot and consider having this conversation with your boss. Feel your body; begin to deepen your breath. Notice if you can rub your hands together and try swallowing a few times. Remind yourself that you're ok. If you feel overwhelmed, take a break and come back to repeat this process. Do this until your body sensations fade away. Trust me, they will. You simply cannot be in an extreme state and relaxed at the same time. Continue this pattern a few more times until you can consider talking with your boss and still feel your body. Perhaps now you will be enlivened by the possibility of the conversation but not overtaken by sweat and jitters. Then maybe propose what you would say to your boss to a trusted friend or partner. Get clear on your words and intentions. Breath. Notice that once the fear processes you are left with the feeling of joyful expectation with subtle anxiety. Then go get that promotion!

Another option for clearing hard or scary or lacking moments is eye movement reprogramming. (If you have experience with eye movement desensitization and reprocessing or EMDR, this works similarly to that modality.) Anchor your mind in a safe, comfortable, resourced, or even joyful moment from the past, a memory that feels good. With your eyes open, look up and to the left with this memory in your mind. Make sure you really feel it in your body. Now consider what has upset you. Pull that into your body as much as you can/want to and look down to the right. Move your eyes back and forth between these two spots: the upper left and the lower right. Do that until you feel yourself shift into a calmer state of breath and body.

For longer-term regulation, rest often and move slowly, deliberately,and mindfully. Spend time in nature; get into water; baths or long showers; try a deprivation tank. Ask yourself when do you feel safe, resourced, calm, and receptive. How do you know when you're safe? Who's with you? Try to recall a time when you were resourced. What was happening then? Think about how you can begin to incorporate more feelings of calm and rest into your current life. What feels good? What feels nourishing and regulating? Listen for the answers.

As you try all of these tools, continue to be open to your own body's intelligence of something totally new and completely yours to emerge. Part of this process is learning how to slow down and listen to your own innate wisdom.

New Beliefs and Maintenance

Now that you've identified stories based on experiences from the past, cleared yourself of excess energy (or rocks!), started to flex your boundary-creating power, created connection to your inner parts and your little-child, notice that you have a lot of extra space within your mind and body for more creating. You can spend this time creating stories that serve you, that heal you, and that feel supportive, aligned, safe and real. Consider the new belief(s) you're calling into your life. This is a new awareness, a new story that you would prefer to embody. Think about how your newfound connection to your worth can impact you positively.

What's a new belief about yourself you would welcome? What does that feel like? Consider what new actions could support this belief and where this new belief lives within you. Can you grow this new belief and its associated sensations? Think about how your new belief will impact the rest of you and how you're now relating to your self-worth and to people.

Notice how your body sits, stands, and moves, with this new awareness. What else would need to shift to allow you to fully live this new awareness into your daily life?

Notice any awareness of resistance, anything that may block you from sensing into your new possibilities. What's the message? What or who is being protected? You might realize you're looking for external validation or permission; you might be having thoughts of "Who am I to want this? How could I deserve this? It feels too far away– given all my obligations, there's no way I could ever get there." Deeply consider what might be creating these thoughts and if they're really coming from you or from external sources that contain no truth.

I'm also holding space for those of you on the other end of the spectrum where you're smiling and feeling broadness through your shoulders. Maybe your spine has grown two inches. The ability to let go and move on is right here and right now and you're ready to move forward! You are totally aligned with who you are, what you want, and who you want to spend time with, and you've gained clarity of your undeniable self-worth.

Maintenance

This book is essentially about the process, the process of unlearning and relearning about your self-worth. During this process, parts of you will pop up and say "It's hard!" I'll validate that it can be challenging when those parts say, "Stop! Don't look there– it's not worth it!" or "You can't."

Take a breath. Tell those parts that you hear them. Thank them for trying to keep you safe and gently turn your focus to the part of you that is ready. While the new thought, action, and/or behavior you're learning to incorporate may feel awkward or hard or even impossible, it's laying the groundwork for you to move forward in a different way. If you continue what's familiar and you still exist in your established patterns, you'll continue to get what you've gotten in the past. All that to say, if you're going to be uncomfortable, you may as well be uncomfortable while you're going in the direction of growth rather than staying stuck in historical trauma-drama or stories that keep you disconnected from living a life of vibrant self-worth. You may as well be uncomfortable but still moving in the direction of eventually standing tall with your shoulders back, your breath easy, your jaw unclenched, your eyes bright and a smile on your face.

If you keep moving forward, eventually you'll have supportive boundaries in place, tools for maintaining your newfound calm, modes of clear and thoughtful communication, and rewarding relationships with yourself and others. You'll be living in a world where you feel your self-worth with every breath and step you take; you'll have clear, accessible, connections to your inner three-year-old, your inner twelve-year-old, your inner thirty-year-old (and so on) selves that are in alignment with who you are now, what you do now, who you associate with, how you work now, and how you eat, relax, play and enjoy life now.

Maybe you're wondering how you would maintain this state of inner connectedness. Honestly, you return to the questions in this book and allow your answers to deepen with every pass. You would extend past this book and explore various healing modalities; maybe you'd find support groups that would ritualize this work for you or find a therapist or coach who specializes in self-worth and codependency. Your desire for change has to be greater than your desire to remain the same. You have to want it! And by "it," I mean growth, self-awareness, change, and believing in yourself and your life.

Once your new toolbox of boundaries, nervous system regulation, and new beliefs are beginning to work for you in a supportive way, TRUST THAT! Take time to congratulate yourself on the wins (and know that there are no small ones). Be proud of your work! Tell a close friend about it, someone who's truly rooting for you. Throw yourself a little dance party in the kitchen with a big smile and cry tears of relief and joy.

A caveat: please do not do not poke at yourself for not being better or further along the path of recovery and self-awareness. Do not talk yourself out of your win because some parts of you don't trust it yet. Easy does it! Frustration may show up, but let it come and go. Allow yourself to continue expanding and celebrate your wins. The process gets way easier as you go along–you'll move through the process more quickly the more you can trust it.

This process is a fine balance of persistence and rest. The work takes a lot of energy: the energy to become aware, the energy to change, the energy to act in new ways. While some days you may feel like burning it all to the ground and starting over fresh, other days you may feel like staying in your bed with the curtains drawn is the best use of your energy. This is certainly not something to force–it's a process. I imagine you have a lot of experience with forcing yourself to tolerate and bend to all types of treatment, but this is different. This process is meant to be a healing one, and that means you're breathing the entire time, you get to practice compassion, you get to take rests, you get to practice patience and grace with yourself, you get to be messy, and you get to be soft and honest with your truth.

Other Healing Modalities

Many resources are available to assist you in your quest to connect with and create new parts in your quest of building your relationship to your self-worth. These tools and resources can look like reading books and listening to podcasts on the subjects of building self-worth, doing inner child work, examining mother/father wounds, digging into codependency, exploring forgiveness, psychedelic psychotherapy, shamanic healing, etc. These tools can also look like EMDR, EFT tapping, meditating, cord cuttings, reiki, shamanic assistance, hypnosis, journaling, massages, acupuncture, essential oils, breath work, communing in nature, vibrational healing, taking naps, dancing, and movement in any form. The list of supportive tools is endless and all are effective at various times in your life.

Some of these things you can do solo; some require assistance from various practitioners. Most of all, you need a willingness to try and listen to what your intuition could be telling you. I say, try what speaks to you, and listen for the results–then you can keep this process growing and deepening for you. You may be someone who doesn't hear their intuition. If that resonates, try a few things from the above list. Ask your friends about their self-care/self-healing rituals and explore what resources alternative healers are offering in your area. Look at bulletin boards at food co-ops, google "healing in my area," and stop by alternative bookstores and ask to see if they know of anyone. Be willing to get woo-woo and see what you learn along the way.

You can also revisit all of the tools in this book. In fact, I urge you to do so for the purposes of deepening your connection to your self-worth. This work is not a one-and-done situation. It's a practice, a refinement of yourself for yourself; it's an opportunity to deeply experience and know your limitless and abundant worth on a core level. Use the tools from this book to work on yourself, seek outside support, and share your time with people who value your presence and want nothing from you.

Eventually, all of this becomes way easier, I promise. The process of identification and clearing becomes second nature, and you can re-source yourself into a place of knowing. I urge you to continue jour-naling—continue getting in touch with younger parts of yourself and supporting them through tough experiences. Continue to be curious and act in ways that support the person you're becoming. Face the shadows and the scary parts and the parts that feel small and afraid. Create supportive boundaries, move your body often, rest often, and surround yourself with people who value you.

Be so, so honest with yourself about your process. There is no rush here—take your time and learn about yourself. What would it be like to accept and love all the parts of yourself? How would you show up differently? Who would be in your life? How would you communicate with your body? Your FOO? Think about what support would feel like and how you can move towards more support. Are you willing to see your self-worth? To believe you're truly worthy, right here, right now? Because you are. If you're having difficulty believing that, know that I believe in you. I know you have inherent worth. No matter what.

Breathe.

About the Author

I recently sat in my own therapy session peeling back yet another layer of my self-awareness in relation to my self-worth. I was able to contact the young child within. She was in deep grief, living in a dark cave within my psyche, small and depleted. As I retrieved her, I realized she was also tired and scared. I was also able to access another part, the part of me that's endlessly nurturing, mothering, and kind. She was beckoning the child to rest in her lap. Then a third part of me emerged. It was the angry one, seething with rage and carrying a message that was so undeniable: the recognition that I wasn't born that way. I was not born fragmented, scared, sad, and unsure of myself. That was a message I was taught, and I learned it in order to survive my childhood.

Now at the ripe age of 42 I get to sit with all of these parts. I get to observe them, feel them, and relate to them, knowing they're all wise and necessary. As the small one rests, she receives the love and validation of her self-worth, taking all the time and reassurance she desires. The nurturing part sits in recognition of her profound gift to love and heal. The angry one finally gets to relax because she was desperately defending the smaller part, and now that the smaller part is receiving love, the angry one gets to see life from a different perspective—one of ease.

I get to walk away from this session vulnerable, open to my own experience and ultimately more integrated within myself, my truth, and my deeply known worth. I have made the unconscious conscious, and there's tremendous power in living with this level of self-awareness.

My childhood wasn't easy and was followed by perhaps even more traumatic teenage years. I experienced sexual abuse at the hands of multiple people including incestual rape. I was emotionally, mentally, and physically abused. Some of this abuse was normalized by my family of origin not because they were bad people, but because they too endured similar and oftentimes worse experiences. Before the age of 21, I was in the rooms of Alcoholics Anonymous, and while I did not remain there, that served as a gateway to my healing. I made many painful choices toward myself and others throughout most of my 20s.

In my 30s, I became a mother and that created a major shift in what I was willing to give and receive. Another major turning point was when I decided to leave an extremely toxic relationship with my children's father and move across the country with our two children to attend grad school and become a somatic psychotherapist. That choice was deeply rooted in knowing that if I stayed in that relationship, I would never be the kind of mother I knew was capable of being and that my children deserved. I knew I would die bitter and a victim. I didn't want that to be my story.

This book is a compilation of the years of work I've done with therapists and healers for myself as well as what I've learned in the process of becoming a therapist myself and the work I've done with clients. Everything I talk about in this book is something I've tried for myself and others. I know it works.

Acknowledgements

Editors:

Rick Bond- You were the very first person to lay eyes on this books roughest of drafts and rooted for it all the way! Thank you for your encouragement and time.

Lisa Howard- Thank you for refining my words to bring more clarity and understanding.

Front Cover Illustration and Formatting:

Very Much So.Agency- Thank you for giving this book its most perfect face! I appreciate your time and detail.

Photography:

Kayla Schmah- Your artistry and grace are beyond exceptional, thank you!

To my friends for your support and celebration of this endeavor. A special shout out to Sarah Knapik for being my closest friend and supporter through this year of uncovering the book I had within. AHO!

Dillon Cruz for being the spark that ignited this heart and the depth that keeps me motivated.

Emma Cruz for showing me the way of endless sweetness, creativity and compassion.

To my family and co-parent, perhaps we never quite know the extent to which we impact the lives of others, please know you have been my greatest of teachers to date and for that I am eternally grateful.

To my own therapist and coach, C.G., you rock my world. Thank you.

To my clients, without you this work would not have been possible. I am in awe of your courage and curiosity. Thank you for trusting me.

Notes

_____

_____

_____

_____

_____

_____

_____

_____

_____

_____

_____

_____

_____

_____

_____

_____

_____

Notes

Notes

Notes

Notes

_____

_____

_____

_____

_____

_____

_____

_____

_____

_____

_____

_____

_____

_____

_____

Notes

Notes

_____

_____

_____

_____

_____

_____

_____

_____

_____

_____

_____

_____

_____

_____

_____

_____

_____

Notes

_____

_____

_____

_____

_____

_____

_____

_____

_____

_____

_____

_____

_____

_____

Notes

Notes